D0789028

WOODLAND PUBLIC LIBRARY

Religions of the World

Judaism

Michael Keene

WORLD ALMANAC® LIBRARY

J
296
Kee
2006

Please visit our web site at: www.worldalmanaclibrary.com
For a free color catalog describing World Almanac® Library's list of high-quality
books and multimedia programs, call 1-800-848-2928 (USA) or 1-800-387-3178
(Canada). World Almanac® Library's fax: (414) 332-3567.

Library of Congress Cataloging-in-Publication Data

Keene, Michael.
    Judaism / by Michael Keene.
        p. cm. — (Religions of the world)
    Includes bibliographical references and index.
    ISBN 0-8368-5869-7 (lib. bdg.)
    ISBN 0-8368-5875-1 (softcover)
    1. Judaism—Juvenile literature. I. Title. II. Religions of the
world (Milwaukee, Wis.)
    BM573.K44   2005
    296—dc22   2005041734

This edition first published in 2006 by
World Almanac® Library
330 West Olive Street, Suite 100
Milwaukee, WI 53212 USA

This edition copyright © 2006 by World Almanac® Library. Original edition copyright © 2005 by
Hodder Wayland. First published in 2005 by Hodder Wayland, an imprint of Hodder Children's Books,
a division of Hodder Headline Limited, 338 Euston Road, London NW1 3BH, U.K.

Consultant: Jonathan Gorsky, The Council of Christians and Jews
Project Editor, Hodder Wayland: Kirsty Hamilton
Editor: Nicola Barber
Designer: Janet McCallum
Picture Researcher: Shelley Noronha, Glass Onion Pictures
Maps and artwork: Peter Bull
World Almanac® Library editor: Gini Holland
World Almanac® Library cover design: Kami Koenig

Photo Credits
The publisher would like to thank the following for permission to reproduce their pictures:
Art Directors/I. Genut 24; Bridgeman Art Library www.bridgeman.co.uk/West London Synagogue,
UK 10, Palazzo Ducale, Urbino, Italy 13, Stapleton Collection, UK 14, Private Collection 25;
CIRCA Photo Library/Barrie Searle 18, 19, 26, 29; Corbis/David Rubinger 9, Hanan Isachar 39,
Alexander Demianchuk/Reuters 43, Reuters 45; Eye Ubiquitous 7; Jewish Museum, Berlin/Jens Ziehe 41;
Robert Harding Picture Library/S. Grandadam 15, ASAP 21, A. Simmenauer 33, Photri 35; Hutchison
Picture Library 5; Alex Keene 23; Ann and Bury Peerless 8, 20; Zev Radovan 28, 36, 44; Topfoto 4, 16,
17, 22, 27, 30, 31, 32, 34, 37, 38, 42; © David H. Wells/Corbis: cover

All rights reserved. No part of this book may be reproduced, stored in a retrieval system, or transmitted
in any form or by any means, electronic, mechanical, photocopying, recording, or otherwise, without
the prior written permission of the copyright holder.

Printed in China

1 2 3 4 5 6 7 8 9 09 08 07 06 05

Contents

Note

In the Western world, years are numbered as either B.C. ("Before Christ") or A.D. ("Anno Domini"—which is Latin for "In the year of our Lord . . ."). In this book, the more neutral terms B.C.E. ("Before the Common Era") and C.E. ("Common Era") are used. The Jewish calendar gives the year of creation as 3760 B.C.E. This means that in the Jewish calendar, the year 2000 C.E. was 5760–5761.

Introduction

The Jewish community goes back thousands of years and today is to be found in most parts of the world. For many Jews, the feeling of belonging to this worldwide community is as important as the sense of sharing a common history with others. In Israel, a Jew is someone who is born to a Jewish mother or who converts to Judaism. Elsewhere, in Conservative and Reform Judaism, children may be raised as Jewish if either parent belongs to the faith.

The Jewish "Family"

To understand the worldwide Jewish community of just over thirteen million people, it helps to think of all Jews as belonging to one, very large "family." The members of this "family" are part of one of the oldest religions in the world, a religion that began over three thousand years ago. They have not, however, always been known by this name. In the beginning, Jews were known as "Israelites" from their ancestor, Jacob (also called Israel). Then they were called "Hebrews" after the nomadic tribe of which they were a part. These two names were later linked to the language that they spoke (Hebrew) and the country in which they lived (Israel). The word "Jew" comes from "Judah," the name of one of the tribes descended from Jacob. Most of these tribes disappeared more than 2,500 years ago, when they were exiled from their homeland (*see page 12*), but the "Judeans" among them later returned.

Belonging to this Jewish "family" means accepting a whole way of life with its own religious and cultural traditions, including special dietary laws and customs. As with any large family, the Jewish family is made up of people with different opinions who like to live and worship in different ways. Some, called "secular Jews," do not actively worship God but may still feel themselves to be part of the Jewish community.

◄ *A Jewish child lights the last candle on the special menorah used during the eight-day festival of Hanukkah* (see page 34*).*

▲ A father and son sit together during worship in a synagogue in London, England. The father is wearing his tallith (prayer shawl), as he does every time he prays in the synagogue (see page 30), and his son wears a kippah (yarmulke, or skullcap) on his head.

In Our Own Words

"All Jews are part of a long, and very proud, religious tradition. We feel a link with all the Jews who have lived, and suffered, back to the time of our father, Abraham. There is no single Jewish way that we all follow. We do what suits us individually in the end. The bottom line is that you do what feels right. To describe Judaism as a 'family' is right. We sometimes have strong disagreements with other members of the 'family' and fall out, but it rarely lasts. I have yet to meet anyone who is not, deep down, proud to be a Jew."

Where Are Jews Found?

Throughout history, Jews have always moved around, often as refugees searching for a new home. As a result they have, over the centuries, settled in most parts of the world.

The Ashkenazim and the Sephardim

There are two main Jewish traditions: the *Ashkenazim* and the *Sephardim*. Ashkenazim refers to Jews from central and eastern Europe. These Jews originally lived in northern France and Germanic cities along the Rhine River. The word *Ashkenazim* comes from the Hebrew name *Ashkenaz* which became associated with an ancient Germanic tribe, the Ascanians, and therefore with the German Jews. The Ashkenazim created their own distinctive culture with their own language—*Yiddish*, a mixture of German, Hebrew, and Slavic dialects. Today, most of the Jews living in the United States are descended from the Ashkenazim, and many others live in Israel and Australia.

The name Sephardim comes from the Hebrew word for Spain. It describes those Jews who were originally from Spain and Portugal, but who fled to North Africa, Greece, Italy, and the Ottoman Empire after being expelled by the Christian rulers of Spain in 1492 (*see page 15*). Like the Ashkenazim, the Sephardim also had their own culture and their own language —*Ladino*, a mixture of Spanish and Hebrew.

These two Jewish groups have their own customs, traditions, liturgy, songs, and prayers. At the same time, they share their most important beliefs.

▼ *This map shows areas with the highest concentrations of Jews throughout the world.*

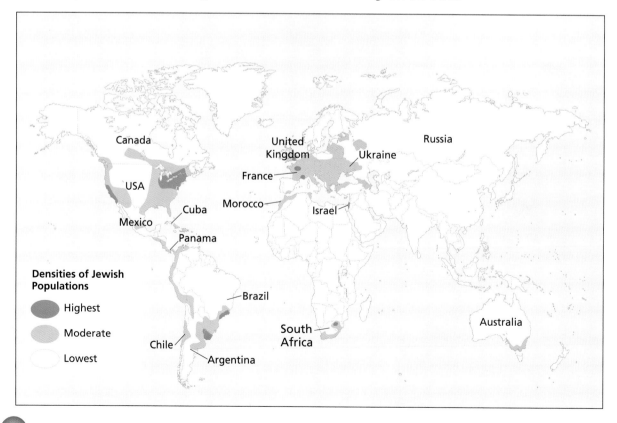

Canada

United Kingdom

Russia

Ukraine

France

USA

Cuba

Morocco

Israel

Mexico

Panama

Densities of Jewish Populations

Highest

Moderate

Lowest

Brazil

Australia

South Africa

Chile

Argentina

The Spread of the Jews

The largest Jewish community in the world is in the United States. There are 5.5 million American Jews, with almost 2 million of this number living in New York. About 4.5 million Jews live in Israel. There has always been a small Jewish community in Palestine (present day Israel), but many European Jews started to move to Palestine in the late nineteenth and early twentieth centuries in response to poverty and persecution. More Jews arrived after the end of the World War II (1939–45), and, after the founding of the state of Israel (1948), Jews came from many different countries. Among them were Jews from Iran and Iraq in the late 1940s and Jews from Ethiopia in the 1980s and 1990s. Jews from Yemen started to settle in Israel as early as the 1880s, but this movement speeded up in the early twentieth century and again after 1948. About 300,000 Jews now live in the United Kingdom (UK), with about 200,000 of them in London and the southeast of England. Despite their reduced and dispersed numbers, Jews have made major contributions to the cultures in which the have lived, especially in the sciences, the arts, education, and politics. Some key world contributors include Albert Einstein, Sigmund Freud, and Jonas Salk.

▲ A shop front in the Jewish Quarter of the Lower East Side in New York displays its name in both Hebrew and Roman alphabets. New York City has a larger Jewish population than any other city in the world.

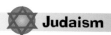

Jewish Groups

Within Judaism there are three main groups: Orthodox, Progressive, and Conservative Jews.

Orthodox Jews

Most Jews in Britain and Israel belong to an Orthodox synagogue. In the United States, however, Orthodox Jews account for only 10 percent of the Jewish population. Orthodox Jews believe that the *Torah*, the first five books of the Bible, is God's eternal word and can never change. In an Orthodox synagogue, men and women sit separately, and the Hebrew language is used in all services. Women do not lead services in Orthodox synagogues. A bar mitzvah service is held for all boys at the age of thirteen to mark their reception as adults into the Jewish community (*see page 37*). For weekday services, men wear the traditional *tefillin* (small leather boxes containing scriptural writings) on their forehead and left arm, as well as a skullcap and a prayer shawl. The Sabbath day is kept strictly as a day of rest, and the kosher rules about food (*see pages 26–27*) are followed throughout the week.

▲ *This man is wearing his* tefillin *and his son is carrying a Torah scroll. The occasion is the boy's bar mitzvah, which is being held at the Western Wall in Jerusalem (see page 15).*

Progressive Jews

Most Progressive Jews belong to Reform or Liberal synagogues, although there are several other groups of Progressive Jews. Both Reform and Liberal Jews believe that Judaism should adapt over time to suit changing circumstances. Progressive Judaism teaches that God guides and judges each person, and that what is right for one person may not be right for another. Men and women sit together in Progressive synagogues, and services are conducted in the everyday language of the worshipers. Women are allowed to be rabbis.

Conservative Jews

The Conservative movement is substantial in the United States and numerically small but lively in Britian. Conservative Jews are traditionally more orthodox than "progressive," but like Reform Jews, they emphasize historical changes and flexibility in Jewish tradition.

➤ *Rabbi Naamah Kelman leads a service in 1992. While services in an Orthodox synagogue can only be led by a male rabbi, women can be rabbis in the Progressive tradition. Naamah Kelman was the first female rabbi to be ordained in Israel, at the Hebrew Union College, Jewish Institute of Religion, in Jerusalem.*

Ten Basic Facts about Judaism

1. Judaism began about four thousand years ago in Mesopotamia, the region in the Middle East that is modern Iraq.

2. Jews worship one God.

3. There are about thirteen million Jews in the world today.

4. A Jewish place of worship is called a synagogue.

5. The Torah is the most important part of the Jewish Scriptures.

6. The scrolls of the Torah, the most precious objects in a synagogue, sit in the Ark—a cabinet at the front of the synagogue.

7. The best-known Jewish symbols are the six-pointed Star of David, or *Magen David* (shield of David), and the *menorah, a* seven-branched candle holder.

8. Jews trace their ancestry back to Abraham, the father of their nation, and to Moses, who gave them their precious Torah.

9. The Sabbath day (*Shabbat*), which starts about half an hour before the beginning of sunset every Friday and is completed when the stars appear in the sky (dusk) on Saturday night, is a day of rest for all Jews.

10. Jews have their own calendar that goes back to what they believe is the day of creation. This calendar is 3,761 years ahead of the Western calendar.

History of the Jews

Judaism can be traced all the way back to Abraham, who lived nearly four thousand years ago, in roughly 1800 B.C.E. He is referred to by Jews today as "our father, Abraham" and is remembered as the person who began the Jewish people. Much later Moses gave the Jews the rules of their faith.

Abraham

Abraham was brought up in the small town of Ur, in southern Mesopotamia, close to the Persian Gulf. Like everyone else at the time, his family worshiped many gods. Abraham, however, came to believe in one God, who created the world and controlled human history. This event marks the beginning of Judaism. At about the same time, God made a promise to Abraham that marked out the Jews as God's "Chosen People"—chosen not because they were better than other people, but because they were different as a result of their relationship with God.

➤ This painting by a twentieth-century artist shows Abraham about to offer his son Isaac as a sacrifice. Jews believe that Abraham's willingness to sacrifice his son—an act that God stopped at the last minute—was a test of Abraham's faith in God. The painting is in the West London Synagogue, UK.

The Patriarchs

Abraham was told by God to travel over 1,240 miles (2,000 kilometers) with his family to a new country, Canaan, now called Israel. God also promised that he would make a great nation out of Abraham's descendants. For years, Abraham's wife Sarah remained childless, although Abraham did have a son, Ishmael (a patriarch of Muslims today), with Sarah's servant, Hagar. Then Sarah gave birth to a son when she was well beyond normal child-bearing age. The child's name was Isaac. Jews believe that they are all descendants of Abraham. He is known as a patriarch, or founding father, of their religion. Abraham's son, Isaac, and his grandson, Jacob, are also revered by Jews as patriarchs.

God's Promise to Abraham

According to the Torah, the holy book of the Jews, this is God's promise to Abraham:

*"I will make you a great nation and I will bless you;
I will make your name great, and you will be a blessing.
I will bless those who bless you, and whoever curses you I will curse, and all peoples on earth will be blessed through you."*

(Genesis 12:2-3)

▼ *This map shows the route taken by Abraham when, according to the Torah, he responded to the call of God to move his extended family to another country.*

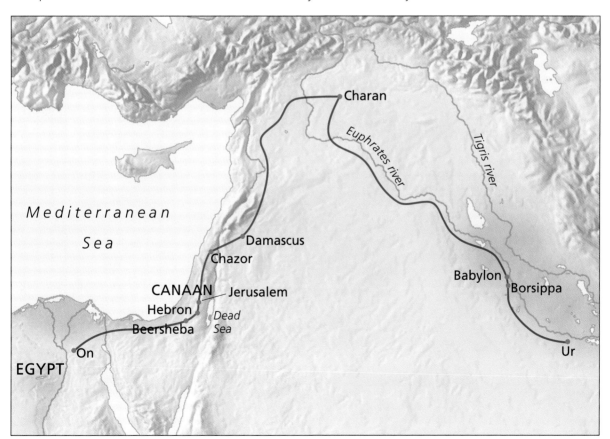

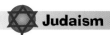

Moses

Throughout history, Jews who are believed to have received messages from God have been called "prophets." The greatest of all the Jewish prophets was Moses, known to Jews as "Moses, our teacher" (*Moshe Rabeinu* in Hebrew). Moses lived about six hundred years after Abraham (*see page 10*).

Ten Plagues

In about 1650 B.C.E., according to the Torah, the Israelites went to Egypt to find food after a famine in Canaan. The Egyptian Pharaoh (king) treated them very badly and forced them to work as slaves. By the time of Moses, the Israelites had been slaves in Egypt for over four hundred years. Moses believed that God was calling him to lead the Israelites out of their slavery, and he told the Pharaoh that many disasters would fall on the Egyptians if the Pharaoh did not release the Israelites. When the Pharaoh refused, ten plagues hit Egypt: The rivers turned to blood; plagues of frogs, lice, and flies covered the land; all of the farm animals died; the people were covered with painful boils; there was a mighty hailstorm; a plague of locusts destroyed the crops; darkness covered the whole land for many days; and, worst of all, the eldest son in every Egyptian family died.

These plagues were believed by many to be punishments from God. After the last one, the Pharaoh released his captives. It took the Israelites forty years to travel back to the land of Canaan (Israel). On this journey in the wilderness, known as the Exodus, the Israelites received some precious laws from God which were given to Moses on Mount Sinai. The most important of these laws are called the Ten Commandments.

▼ *This map shows the route taken by the Israelites when they left Egyptian slavery and traveled to the "Promised Land" of Canaan. The journey took them forty years to complete.*

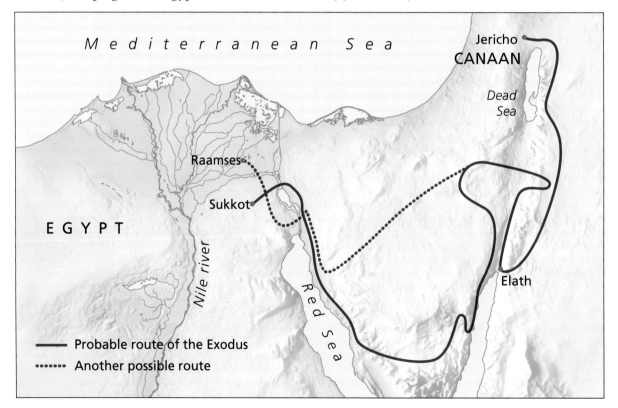

The Ten Commandments

The Ten Commandments form the basis of the Jewish faith. They also contain basic laws that are followed, in one way or another, by most societies. They are:

1. *I am the Lord your God. You must obey no other gods but me.*

2. *You must not make any idols to worship.*

3. *You must not take God's name in vain (use it carelessly or disrespectfully).*

4. *You must remember to keep the Sabbath day holy.*

5. *You must respect your mother and father and obey them.*

6. *You must not murder.*

7. *You must not commit adultery.*

8. *You must not steal.*

9. *You must not tell lies or spread rumors about other people.*

10. *You must not covet (want something that does not belong to you).*

▼ *Moses proclaims the Ten Commandments, which he received from God on Mount Sinai. The Commandments were written in Hebrew on stone tablets. This painting is by a fifteenth-century Dutch artist, Joos van Gent.*

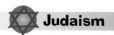

Later Jewish History

There were several tribes in Canaan, each one controlling a small part of the country, so there were many battles before the Israelites finally re-established themselves. The threat of warfare with one of these tribes, the Philistines, led the Israelites to choose a king, Saul, to lead them. He was followed by a succession of kings, including David and Solomon, David's son. Solomon was famed for his great wisdom, especially in settling disputes. He built a magnificent Temple in Jerusalem in which to worship God.

After Solomon died, Canaan was divided into two parts, Israel and Judah. It was the people living in Judah who became known as Jews. In 722 B.C.E., Israel was conquered by the Assyrians, and, in 586 B.C.E., Judah fell to the Babylonians. The old Temple was destroyed and the inhabitants of both Israel and Judah were taken into exile, where they remained for centuries. The communities of Jews that settled outside Israel later became known as the *Diaspora*.

Over the following centuries, Jews gradually began to return to their homeland. In 63 B.C.E., Judah was occupied and ruled by the Romans. At first, the Romans allowed the Jews religious freedom, but later they tried to crush Jewish power and influence. In 70 C.E., they destroyed the rebuilt Jewish Temple and prevented the Jews from living in—or even

▼ *This fifteenth-century woodcut, by the German artist Hartmann Schedel, shows the walled city of Jerusalem with the Temple of Solomon at its center.*

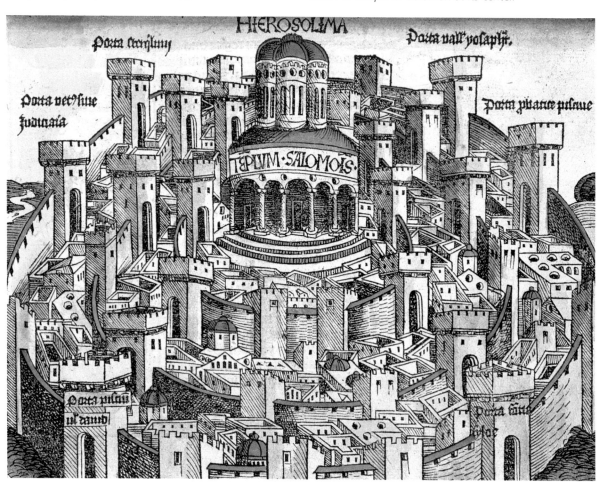

entering—Jerusalem. They also outlawed Jewish education and killed any Jews who continued to teach their young. Most of the Jews fled into exile again.

New Lands

In the centuries that followed, groups of Jews settled in many different countries. With their different religion and clothing style, Jews were often mistrusted by their new neighbors, and this mistrust frequently led to hatred and persecution. The Jews had two things left from their history—their God and their traditions. These were important, not only for religious reasons but also for Jewish pride and survival. To other people, however, Jews often seemed different, dangerous, and threatening.

Christian countries were often the worst places for Jews to live. Jews were persecuted by having their property confiscated, by expulsion, and sometimes by death. Jews were expelled from England in 1290, for example, and from parts of France in 1306. Jews prospered in Muslim Spain for many centuries, but this was followed by a time of intolerance and oppression. In 1492, the Spanish Jews were told by the Christian rulers of Spain either to convert to Christianity or to leave Spain. Thousands left—many to start a new life in Istanbul (in present-day Turkey), where they were welcomed by the Muslim Ottoman rulers. Some Jews, however, chose to stay in Spain and pretend that they were Christian converts. When the Christian authorities discovered what was happening, they set up special courts as part of what was called the Inquisition. These courts used torture and death to try to force the remaining Jews to give up their religious beliefs.

More persecution continued in the centuries that followed. For example, in the nineteenth century, Russian Jewish families were often forced to leave their homes and settle elsewhere in hostile and dangerous parts of Russia. All of this history helps form the background to the unspeakable horrors that were visited on the Jewish people during the Holocaust in the twentieth century.

The Temple of Solomon

The Temple that Solomon built in Jerusalem was magnificent. About 180,000 people were involved in its construction, and its dedication ceremony lasted for fourteen days. It was the place where the three most important Jewish festivals—Pesach, Sukkot, and Shavuot—were celebrated. It was destroyed in 586 B.C.E., although a much larger Temple, built by Herod the Great, replaced it until that, too, was destroyed in 70 C.E. The Temple has never been rebuilt.

▲ *The only wall of Herod's Temple that still remains standing in Jerusalem is one of the holiest sites in Judaism. It is known as the Western Wall.*

The Holocaust

In Germany in the 1930s, Jews once more faced persecution and danger. The Chancellor of Germany, Adolf Hitler, hated the Jews and used them as a convenient scapegoat on which to blame every problem faced by his country.

Although persecution of Germany's Jewish population began before World War II (1939–45), Hitler's program to rid his country and the world of all Jews was put into operation during the war. Hitler called his systematic death plan "The Final Solution."

Hitler's persecution of the Jews had several distinct stages. At first, all Jews had to register at a local office and wear a yellow Star of David on their clothes, so that they could be easily identified. Then he began an attack on the human rights and freedoms of Jews— their businesses were destroyed, they were not permitted to own cars, and their children were not allowed to go to school. Forced to move into guarded ghettos (walled-in areas of towns and cities), Jews lived in overcrowded conditions, often with insufficient food. Many Jews were sent to concentration camps, places of forced labor, where thousands of people died from ill-treatment and lack of food. In the final stage of Hitler's "program," his Nazis rounded up any remaining Jews they could find, young and old, and brought them to death camps—places of mass murder.

By the end of World War II, six million Jews, including one million children, had been killed. This time of horrific persecution and death became known as the Holocaust— "a time of raging fire."

▼ *Jews in the ghetto in Warsaw, Poland, surrender to German soldiers after an uprising against the Nazis in 1943. About 40,000 Jews died during this rebellion.*

▼ *An Israeli soldier arrests a Palestinian demonstrator. Conflict between the Israelis and the Palestinians has continued since the state of Israel was set up in 1948.*

The State of Israel

During the nineteenth century, Jews had begun to resettle in their old homeland of Palestine. A group of Jews called Zionists began to campaign for a separate Jewish state to be set up within Palestine. The Holocaust led to a renewed determination for this plan. On May 14, 1948, the British (who had led both Arabs and Jews to believe they would each have the right to Palestine) gave up control, and the United Nations recognized the modern state of Israel. Jews from all over the world began to travel to this new country to make their home.

The creation of Israel out of Palestine inevitably inflamed growing hostility between Israelis and non-Jewish Palestinians (mainly Muslim Arabs), and between Israel and the surrounding countries, which were also mainly Muslim and Arab. The Israelis were not willing to give up any of the land that many Jews believed God had given them thousands of years ago. On the other hand, most of the Arab countries did not even recognize the right of the state of Israel to exist. Efforts to find a lasting solution to the Arab-Israeli conflict continue today, but so far with only limited success.

2 Beliefs and Holy Books

J ews believe in one invisible, eternal God. They also believe that they have a special relationship with God and were chosen by him to receive the Torah—the first five books of the Jewish Bible, or Scriptures. By studying its teachings and putting them into practice, they hope to spread peace and justice in the world. Jews believe that life in this world is very precious and that the destination of the journey of life is a life after death.

God

The first Hebrew that most Jewish children learn is the *Shema (see page 19)*, which is both a prayer and a statement of faith. The words of the Shema are taken from the Scriptures. They underline the Jewish belief that there is only one God who created the world and sees and knows everything. God is close to everyone and everything. Jews have a word to describe this closeness: *Shekhina*. The *Talmud*, a Jewish holy book, says: "There is no place without the Shekhina." Jews repeat the Shema twice each day—first thing in the morning and last thing at night.

▼ *A Jewish woman shields her eyes as she prays, as a mark of respect to God.*

The Covenant

Jews have always believed that they have a special and unique relationship with God. According to the Jewish Scriptures, this relationship is built on a covenant, or agreement, that was made between God and Abraham thousands of years ago. God promised to be Israel's God and give the Israelites a country of their own. In return, God told the Israelites to dedicate themselves to him alone and to his service and not to worship any other gods.

Later, God renewed this covenant with Abraham's son, Isaac, and with Isaac's son, Jacob who was also called Israel. Although the Jews are sometimes known as the "Chosen People," this special relationship is one of service, not privilege—Jews believe they have been called by God to fulfill his commandments and to be a blessing to the world.

The Shema

The Shema is a combination of three passages taken from the Torah: "Hear, O Israel, the Lord is our God. You shall love the Lord your God with all your heart, with all your soul, and with all your mind. These words which I command you this day you shall take to heart. You shall teach them diligently to your children. You shall recite them when you are at home and when you are away, morning and night. You shall bind them as a sign on your hand, they shall be a reminder above your eyes and you shall inscribe them on the door posts of your home and on your gates."

➤ *The Ten Commandments, written here in Hebrew on the wall of a synagogue in Safed, Israel, act as a reminder to every worshiper of the importance of these precious laws.*

"Teaching"

The word "Torah" means "teaching"— all the things that God has told the Jewish people—and it is at the heart of Jewish life and worship. The word refers primarily to the first five books (also referred to as the Five Books of Moses) of the Jewish Scriptures and contains stories about the early history of the Jewish people, commandments and rules, poems, and sayings about life.

The Torah is divided into portions for each week of the year so that it is read in the synagogue in a never-ending cycle from beginning to end throughout the year. Studying the Torah is a very important part of Jewish life. The text of the Torah is the Jew's link with God. The role of the Jewish rabbi is to teach the Torah, since it is both the source of holiness and eternal life.

▼ When not in use, the scrolls of the Torah are stored in the Ark— a cabinet situated at the front of every synagogue. The scrolls are the most precious objects in a synagogue.

The Giving of the Torah

A much-loved Jewish legend describes how, when the Torah was given to the people by God on Mount Sinai, the mountain itself burst into flower, the birds stopped singing, and the whole universe became quiet and still—as if waiting for something very beautiful to happen. Then followed thunder, lightning, and a thick cloud that covered the whole mountain. God came down on to the mountain in fire and the area shuddered. Such, explains the legend, is the power of the Torah.

▲ *The scrolls of the Torah are handwritten in Hebrew by specially trained scribes.*

The Messiah

The idea of the Messiah comes from the Jewish Bible. The word means "the anointed one" and comes from the ancient practice of anointing kings with oil when they were crowned. The Bible looks forward to a new king for the Jews who will be even greater than the much-loved King David (*see page 14*). Orthodox Jews are still waiting for this king, who will make everything right on Earth, while Progressive Jews look for a new age of love and peace. Many Jews pray each day for their Messiah to come.

The Afterlife

The Bible teaches Jews how they should live in this life. The Jewish Scriptures also make it clear that there is a life after death. They teach that when a person dies, his or her soul survives in *Sheol*, a place of darkness and shadows. God will reward those who have lived a righteous life and punish those who have been sinners—both in this life and in the life beyond death. When God's promised Messiah comes to set up his kingdom on earth, then, according to Jewish belief, the righteous will be brought back to life.

The Jewish Holy Books

The Jewish Bible, or *Tenakh*, is the holy book for all Jews. The Tenakh is a very old collection of writings which falls into three sections: the Torah (teachings), the Prophets (*Nevi'im*), and the Writings (*Ketuvim*; songs and sayings). The sections are divided into different parts, called books. There are thirty-nine books altogether in the Jewish Scriptures. The Torah, for instance, includes the five books of Genesis, Exodus, Leviticus, Deuteronomy, and Numbers.

The Tenakh contains many different kinds of writing. It recounts the history of the Jews from the creation of the world to the time when they were exiled from their homeland of Israel. There are many songs, poems, and wise sayings that arise from this story. The main theme running through the Tenakh, however, is how God loved and guided the Jews, saving them many times from their enemies but also punishing them when they deliberately disobeyed him. Alongside this is a record of the laws and rules that Jews try to follow to please and honor God.

The Torah

The Jews value the first part of their Bible—the Torah—very highly. The books that make up the Torah are a mixture of early Jewish history and laws. The Torah contains the stories about the creation of the world and

▼ *A scroll of the Torah is spread out on the* bimah *in a synagogue in Havana, Cuba, to be read as part of worship. To read from the Torah is a great honor.*

◄ *This stained glass window, in a synagogue in Great Britiain, illustrates the festival of Simchat Torah. The interlocking triangles of the Star of David shine above it, to the right.*

early Jewish history ending with the death of Moses. It also has hundreds of rules covering such matters as cleanliness and diet as well as the Ten Commandments (*see page 13*).

Simchat Torah

The annual festival of *Simchat Torah* gives Jews the opportunity to thank God for his great gift of the Torah to them. Over the course of the year the whole of the Torah, from start to finish, is read in the synagogue on the Sabbath day. Simchat Torah is the day when the last part of the last book, Deuteronomy, is read. The reading then starts again beginning with the first chapter of the first book, Genesis. There is no break between the two readings to show that God's word, the Torah, is eternal, without beginning or end.

In Our Own Words

"As a Jew, the Torah means a great deal to me. The commandments that I find in the Torah are my everyday guide to living. I am able to identify with many of the characters in the Torah, especially Abraham and Moses. They strike me as being real people with many faults and their good points as well. I do not think that the Torah lays down impossible standards for me to reach. It tells me how I should treat other people as if they really matter. It lays down a way of life that I want to follow."

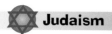

The Prophets and the Writings

Although not as important as the Torah, the Prophets and the Writings are essential parts of the Jewish Scriptures.

The Prophets

A prophet was a human being, male or female, who had been chosen by God to act as his messenger and to make his will known to the people. A prophet was someone who spoke on God's behalf. Although the prophets sometimes made pronouncements about the future, they mostly spoke out about the evils of the present time that displeased God. Many of those evil deeds were being carried out by kings and religious leaders of the time, so the prophets needed great courage to challenge them. The term "prophet" is also used of the Jewish writers whose words and sayings can be found in the prophetic books of the Jewish Bible. These prophets declared God's judgement on human sin and his willingness to save and restore the fortunes of the obedient.

Some of the prophetic books take their name from the prophet whose message is in the book. For example, there are books named after Isaiah, Jeremiah, and Ezekiel. The books of these prophets are long and important. There are also twelve books named after less important prophets such as Hosea, Obadiah, Jonah, and Malachi. These books are much shorter.

◄ An engraving of the prophet Isaiah by the nineteenth-century French artist Gustav Doré, whose illustrations were often used in Jewish Bibles. This picture is in the Tel Aviv Museum in Israel.

The Writings

The Writings are a collection of poems, songs, and wise sayings that make up the final part of the Tenakh. The most popular of these writings is the Book of Psalms, a collection of 150 songs that were used in worship in the Temple. King David and his son, Solomon, are believed to have written many of them. The psalms are notable for the honesty of their writers when they describe their feelings about God and their enemies. Another important book in Writings is the Book of Proverbs, a collection of many wise sayings. King Solomon is also thought to be the author of many, if not all, of these.

▲ *King Solomon and the Queen of Sheba appear on this nineteenth-century Jewish rug, made in Kashan, Persia (present-day Iran). Solomon became famous for his great wisdom and, according to tradition, wrote three books of the Jewish Bible—Ecclesiastes, the Book of Proverbs, and the Song of Solomon.*

From the Psalms

In this psalm the writer is bitter about God. He feels he has been deserted by the Almighty:

"My God, my God, why
   have you forsaken me?
Why are you so far from
   saving [me],
So far from the words
   of my groaning?
O my God, I cry out day by
   day, but you do not answer,
By night and [I] am not silent."
(Psalm 22:1–2)

*In this psalm the writer
   shows a deep faith in God:*

"The Lord is my shepherd,
   I shall not be in want.
He makes me lie down in
   green pastures
He leads me beside still waters,
He restores my soul."

(Psalm 23:1–3)

3 Worship, the Synagogue, and Holy Days

J ews do not have to go to the synagogue to worship God. They can express their faith in the way they live their everyday lives, especially in their family life and in how they behave in the wider world. The way that Jews live is a very important part of belief and worship. They believe that life itself is a gift from God and that everyday activities such as eating a meal or going to bed offer opportunities for praising God. It is said that for every human activity there is a Jewish prayer to be offered to God.

The Mezuzah

The mezuzah is a tiny scroll made out of parchment on which is written the first two paragraphs of the Shema (*see page 19*). Mezuzah scrolls are placed inside small wooden or plastic casings and attached to the right-hand door posts of every room in the house—apart from bathrooms and lavatories. A mezuzah is also placed on the outside door post. As traditional Jews enter and leave their house, they touch the mezuzah and kiss their fingers. This reminds them of the promise in the Torah: "You are blessed when you come in and blessed when you go out" (Deuteronomy 28:6).

Dietary Laws

The word *kosher* means that which is "allowed" or "suitable." Most Orthodox Jews eat only kosher food, but other Jews may not be so strict. The laws that lay down the restrictions observed by Jews are

➤ *The mezuzah attached to the door post of a Jewish home is a reminder of the holiness of the house and God's presence in it.*

to be found in the Torah. The main restrictions are listed here:

- The meat of any animal that does not both chew the cud and have cloven hooves is forbidden. The best known example of forbidden meat is the pig.

- Jews do not eat any sea creature that does not have fins and scales.

- Only birds known to be kosher, such as chicken, duck, and turkey, are permitted.

- All animals must be slaughtered according to strict laws, with all of the blood drained from the carcass before it can be eaten.

- Meat and milky foods must not be eaten together. It is the practice to wait for several hours before eating milky foods after meat has been eaten. Meat and milk are kept separately in the refrigerator and cooked in different containers.

In Our Own Words

"I am not sure that I understand all of the kosher rules and the reasons for them. When I asked the rabbi at my synagogue to explain them to me he said that there were two reasons for the original rules. The first was to maintain a high level of hygiene when our ancestors were traveling across the desert. The second, and most important, is a matter of obedience to God. We may not understand everything that God tells us to do, but that is when we need to trust most strongly."

◄ A kosher butcher in a department store in Austin, Texas. Every kosher butcher's shop is examined by the Jewish religious authorities and given a certificate to state that its meat is kosher—fit to be eaten by Jews who choose to follow Jewish dietary laws.

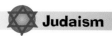

Keeping the Sabbath Day

Shabbat, the Sabbath day, is the Jewish holy day of rest and the only weekly festival in Judaism. It reminds all Jews of two things: that God rested after creating the world in six days and that God delivered the Israelites from slavery in Egypt (*see page 12*).

The Sabbath Day

Each Jewish day of twenty-four hours starts at sunset in the evening and runs to sunset in the next evening. So the Jewish Sabbath begins on Friday evening and finishes at sunset on Saturday evening. On Friday, before the onset of the Sabbath, the house is cleaned and tidied and a special meal is prepared. When the Sabbath day begins, no work of any kind is allowed. The meal is an important family and religious occasion.

For many Jewish families the Sabbath day begins when the mother of the house, who is called "the foundation of the home," lights two or more candles and says a prayer to welcome the holy day. Young children usually stay at home to help their mother, but the father and older children start the Sabbath day in the synagogue. In Conservative and Progressive synagogues, however, the whole family may attend the service. Everyone returns home for the meal, during which the father blesses his children.

➤ *A Jewish mother and her daughter light the candles that mark the beginning of the Sabbath day. When the male members of their family return home from the service in the synagogue, their family will eat the Shabbat meal together.*

Just as the Sabbath day begins with prayer and ceremony, so the day ends Saturday at sunset with a special ceremony. Traditionally, this takes place as soon as three stars can be seen clearly in the sky. The Sabbath day is brought to a close with Havdalah ("the

separation"), a ceremony that draws a clear line between the holiness of the Sabbath day and the ordinariness of the week ahead. Blessings are given over wine, spices, and a plaited candle, as everyone exchanges wishes for a good and "sweet-smelling" week ahead.

Forbidden Activities on the Sabbath Day

Many activities are forbidden for Orthodox Jews on the Jewish holy day. They include light- ing a fire, cooking, switching on any electrical equipment, playing a musical instrument, driving a car, using public transportation—such as a bus, train, or airplane—writing, watching television, or riding a bicycle or a motorcycle.

◄ *This ornate silver holder contains sweet spices such as cinnamon, cloves, nutmeg, and bay leaves. It is used during the Havdalah ceremony, which marks the end of the Sabbath day and the separation of the holy day from the world of work.*

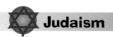

Worship in the Synagogue

As Jews enter a synagogue, a place for "meeting together," some may wash their hands to make them fit to worship God before saying a prayer: "I will worship facing towards your holy Temple. Lord, I love the dwelling of your house and the place where your glory rests." In many Orthodox synagogues, there must be a minimum of ten men present in the synagogue before a service can go ahead. In Reform or other Progressive synagogues where this rule is observed, women are included in the total.

Special Clothes

Many Orthodox Jewish men wear a skullcap (kippah) all of the time, both inside and outside the synagogue. In Orthodox synagogues men also wear over their clothes a special rectangular prayer shawl, or tallith, which is usually made of wool or silk. The tallith has a fringe and tassels at both ends to help worshipers remember the 613 commandments found in the Torah. For weekday services in the synagogue, Orthodox Jewish men wear two small leather boxes called tefillin, which are tied with leather straps in the middle of the forehead and on the left arm. Like a mezuzah (*see page 26*), these boxes carry the first two paragraphs of the Shema written on parchment scrolls, reminding each worshiper that the word of God should be carried in one's mind and heart.

The words inside a tefillin can be written only by trained scribes using special materials. Once every three years, a tefillin should be opened by a rabbi and the words checked. If the parchment is undamaged, then the words can be corrected if they have become difficult to read. If, however, the parchment scroll has been damaged or if it is cracked, then it must be replaced.

▼ *Talliths hang on a rack in the New Haven Hebrew Day School, Orange, Connecticut. A tallith is a very important personal possession, and many Jewish men are buried with their talliths when they die.*

The Rabbi

A rabbi is a person who is well respected in the Jewish community because he or she is highly trained in the Torah as well as in Jewish law and tradition. Most rabbis are the spiritual leaders of Jewish congregations. In Orthodox synagogues, a rabbi is always male, but in Reform, Conservative, and other synagogues, rabbis can be either male or female. The rabbi takes part in Sabbath worship by leading prayers, reading from the Torah, and giving a sermon. He or she also conducts weddings, funerals, and classes to educate members of the community about their religion, as well as visiting the sick and the bereaved.

Three rabbis in an area form a Bet Din. *This is a court of Jewish law. This court authorizes marriages and conversions, resolves disputes, and interprets matters of Jewish law. It also plays an important part in granting a bill of divorce, called a* get, *to Jewish couples who want to split up. The get provides couples with a "religious" divorce that means that they can remarry in a synagogue. Without this, their remarriage is not religiously recognized.*

▼ *As leaders in the Jewish community, rabbis play many roles. Here Rabbi Yaakov Rapoport and his helpers knead and roll matzoh in a model bakery in a Jewish Community Center in the United States. The matzoh, unleavened bread, plays an important part in the celebration of Passover.*

Jewish Festivals

There are many Jewish festivals that are celebrated throughout the year. Among the main festivals are Rosh Hashanah, Yom Kippur, Sukkot, Shavuot, Hanukkah, Purim, and Pesach (Passover).

Rosh Hashanah

Rosh Hashanah, the Jewish New Year, marks the start of the holiest period on the Jewish calendar. It begins the Ten Days of Penitence that end on Yom Kippur (the Day of Atonement). It is a time for Jews to reflect on their behavior in the past year and to try to right any wrongs they may have done. During Rosh Hashanah, a ram's horn, called a *shofar*, is blown one hundred times in the synagogue to call the people to repent of their sins. There are three basic sounds blown: a long, drawn-out note; briefer notes; and very short notes. The sound of the shofar reminds many Jews of a person crying and helps them to reflect on their own sins and shortcomings.

Yom Kippur

Yom Kippur, a day of prayer and fasting and the most solemn day of the year, lasts for twenty-five hours and draws the Ten Days of Pentitence to a close. On this day, Jews follow the example of God's angels who, according to traditional belief, do not eat or drink. Jews spend the time in prayer and confession, asking God's forgiveness and seeking the forgiveness of their friends and relations.

▼ *A rabbi, preparing for Rosh Hashanah, practices blowing a shofar.*

➤ *This booth, built for the festival of Sukkot in Jerusalem, is a public booth, but many people construct and decorate their own family booths to celebrate this festival.*

Sukkot

Sukkot is a very happy Jewish festival for which many families build a booth in their yard. This booth is a hut decorated with flowers and fruit, with a roof made of leaves and branches. Many families eat their meals in the booth, and some even sleep in it. The booth is a symbol of trust in the God who protected the Israelites during forty years of traveling in the wilderness (*see page 12*). During synagogue services, people wave palm branches, myrtle, and willow leaves, as well as a type of citrus fruit called an *etrog* (used as an early Jewish symbol) to show that God is everywhere.

Shavuot

Shavuot is a summer festival that celebrates the anniversary of God giving the Torah to Moses. Jews decorate their synagogues with lots of flowers to remind worshipers of the tradition that Mount Sinai burst into flower when the Torah was given by God (*see page 20*). This festival is also known as the Feast of Weeks because it falls seven weeks after the first day of Passover (a "week of weeks").

In Our Own Words

"I love Sukkot because I enjoy building a booth in the yard with my parents, brother, and sister. The most important festival, though, is Pesach because of what it means for all Jews. It's the festival of freedom. We remember that God brought all of our ancestors out of Egypt—the place of slavery. We need to remember that we are descended from slaves, as this makes us appreciate our freedom. Seder night is a big family meal where we read the Passover story out loud. This is a night for Jews to put aside their disputes and join together as a family."

Hanukkah

This festival, also known as the Festival of Light, celebrates the victory of a Jewish family called the Maccabees over the armies of the Greek Syrian king, Antiochus Epiphanes, in the second century B.C.E. The king's forces had defiled the Temple, making it unfit for worship. When the Temple was retaken, the Jews decided to hold a dedication ceremony. There was only one flask of oil for lighting the lamp that burns in front of the Ark (*see page 9*)—only enough oil for one night. Miraculously, it lasted for eight days—enough time for new oil to be prepared. To commemorate both the rebellion and the miracle, on each day of Hanukkah a candle is lit on a special menorah, until all eight are shining on the last night (*see picture, page 4*). During this festival, children play a Hanukkah game with a spinning top called a dreidel, and families eat special potato pancakes called latkes.

Purim

Purim celebrates the story of Esther, who foiled a plot to destroy the Jews of Persia about 2,500 years ago. This is an exciting festival for children. In the synagogue, the story behind the festival is read aloud from a decorated scroll, and children dress up in the costumes of the characters. Every time the name Haman (the villain in the story) is mentioned, the children make as much noise as possible, using whistles, rattles, and garbage can lids, or by just stamping their feet. They are trying to blot out the name of Haman by their noise.

Passover

Passover (Pesach), which commemorates events that took place over 3,000 years ago, is the most important of all the Jewish festivals. The freedom of people everywhere is the theme of this festival, because the Israelites had been slaves in Egypt for over four hundred years when God

◄ *These children in Jerusalem, dressed up for the festival of Purim, parade through the streets before going into the synagogue to hear the story read aloud. The costumes represent characters from the Biblical story of Esther.*

miraculously delivered them (*see page 12*). The word "Passover" refers to the time when the Angel of Death passed over the houses of the Jews, who had marked their doors with lamb's blood. The Angel of Death spared the Jews but delivered plagues on the Egyptians until the Pharaoh released the Jewish slaves. The main part of Passover is a special meal, the *seder*, during which the story of the Israelites' slavery and escape is told. The seder plate contains different foods, each with a symbolic meaning (*see box*). They are eaten as the story is told to help people share in the original experience. Jews also eat unleavened bread (matzoh) to remind them that when the Israelites left Egypt, they did not have time to let their bread rise. At the close of the seder, the participants proclaim in unison, "Next year in Jerusalem" to express the hope that all people will one day be free.

▼ *Most of the food on the seder plate is eaten during the Passover service to remind worshipers of what happened to the early Israelites.*

The Seder Plate

The seder plate on the table holds a number of different food items to remind everyone of the meaning of Passover. Two of them, a roasted egg and a roasted lamb bone, commemorate worship in the old Temple, but they are not eaten. Among those that are eaten are bitter herbs, a reminder of the bitter lives of the slaves; one or two green vegetables to remind everyone that this is a spring festival; and a mixture of chopped apples, nuts, cinnamon, and wine to symbolize the cement used by the Israelite slaves when they were building houses for their Egyptian masters.

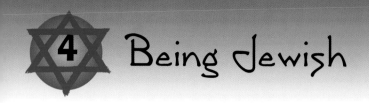
Being Jewish affects a person's whole life, from the moment of birth until the time of death. There are Jewish ceremonies or rituals to mark all of the important times in a person's life.

Circumcision

Circumcision is the oldest Jewish religious practice that is still carried out today. It goes all the way back to Abraham, who was told by God to circumcise all the male members of his family. Circumcision has always been carried out on the eighth day after a boy's birth. The ceremony must take place on that day even if it falls on the Sabbath, since only illness is allowed to delay it. The ceremony, in which the foreskin of a boy's penis is removed, is carried out in the child's home—or in the synagogue—by a mohel, who does not need to be a rabbi or a doctor but must be a specially trained religious Jew.

▼ *A Jewish baby boy is circumcised. The operation is performed by a trained person called a mohel and is usually watched by all the members of the family, except the child's mother.*

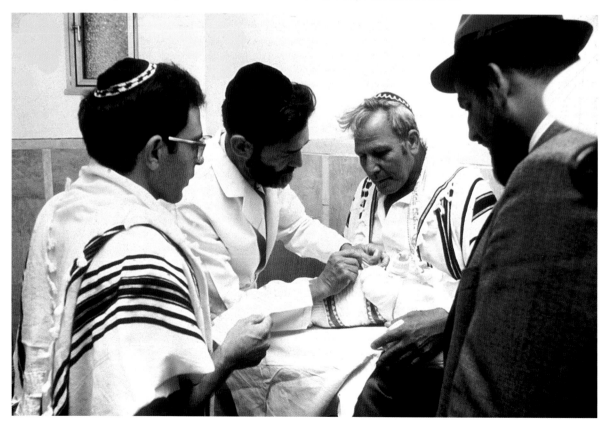

Bar Mitzvah

Bar Mitzvah marks a boy's entry into adulthood. It is held on the first Sabbath day after a boy's thirteenth birthday, by which time he must be able to read Hebrew well. Until this point in the boy's life, the child's father has been responsible for his son's spiritual welfare and ensuring that the Jewish laws are obeyed. Now this responsibility is passed to the boy himself. As part of his Bar Mitzvah service, a boy must be able to read a passage from the Torah scroll in Hebrew. He also leads the congregation in their prayers.

Bat Mitzvah

Girls join adult Jewish society a year earlier than boys. In some non-Orthodox synagogues they have a similar ceremony, called *Bat Mitzvah*, in which girls read from the Torah. In many Orthodox synagogues there is a ceremony for girls in which, although they do not read publicly from the Torah, they do give a special talk about the Torah reading for that week.

In Our Own Words

"I have just celebrated my Bar Mitzvah. I learned Hebrew in our classes at the synagogue—although it is frightening to stand up in front of all your relations and friends to read from the Torah in a language that is not your native tongue! I'd practiced it a lot, however, and all went well. The service was followed by a special meal at which everyone gave me presents—that was very nice! I stood up to thank them for their love and kindness as well as telling them my hopes for a Jewish future. I want to be able to keep as many of the Jewish laws as possible, to live a life that is faithful to God, and to establish my own Jewish home in the years to come."

◄ *A Bar and Bat Mitzvah class is held for both boys and girls in a Conservative synagogue in Tel Aviv, Israel. In this class, children are taught Hebrew as well as more about their Jewish faith.*

Marriage

Marriage is very important to all Jews. Although a Jewish marriage, for which both bride and groom have to be Jewish, does not have to take place in a synagogue, it is most likely to be held in a place of worship.

During the wedding service, the bride and groom stand together under a *chuppah* (canopy) which is sometimes decorated with white flowers. This canopy is a symbol of the home that the couple are going to set up together. The couple drink wine together as the wedding blessings are recited. The groom gives his bride a ring and formally takes her in marriage. In Reform and other Progressive services, the bride takes the groom in marriage as well. Then the *ketubah*, the marriage certificate, is read aloud and signed before the groom crushes a wine glass beneath his feet. This is an ancient practice recalling the destruction of the Temple, which Jews remember even in times of great joy.

Judaism encourages a Jew to marry someone who is also Jewish. Many Jews believe that Judaism is so centered around home life that unless a married couple share the same religious background and beliefs, it will be very difficult for them to live together in true harmony.

▼ *A Jewish couple embrace beneath a* chuppah *at their wedding.*
A Jewish wedding can take place outdoors, in the synagogue, or in the home.

Death

Jewish tradition demands that a Jewish funeral and burial take place as soon as possible after death—ideally within 24 hours. Funeral services must be simple, with the body being placed in a basic coffin. This is because Jews believe that everyone, rich and poor, is equal in death since there is no difference between them in the eyes of God. Orthodox Jews do not allow cremation, although it is permitted by Progressive Jews.

For a week after the burial, friends and relations meet in the home of the dead person to comfort one another. During this time, close relatives of the deceased are not expected to go to work or to do anything in the home so that they can grieve without worrying about the everyday details of their lives. Friends and relations support them in every way. For almost a year, close relatives recite the *kaddish*, a holy prayer, every day. A special candle is lit each year on the anniversary of the person's death.

The Kaddish

This prayer praises God, who is the giver of all life. It is read at times of both joy and sorrow: "Let us magnify and let us sanctify the great name of God in the world, which he created according to his will. May his kingdom come in your lifetime, and in your days, and in the lifetime of the family of Israel— quickly and speedily may it come— He is far beyond any blessing or song, any honor or any consolation that can be spoken of in this world."

▼ *A girl lights a memorial candle at the grave of the assassinated Israeli Prime Minister, Yitzak Rabin.*

Judaism is a very old religion. Like other religions, however, it needs to be able to face modern problems in the world. To do this, Judaism takes the principles of the Torah and tries to see how those principles can be applied today.

Justice for Everyone

Jews believe that God gave all people the laws they need to live good and honest lives when he gave Moses the Torah on Mount Sinai. The Torah contains everything that Jews need to know about how they should behave and what is expected of them by God. A legal code has been drawn up from the Torah by rabbis over the centuries, and this is called the *Halakhah*. Jews believe that these laws can bring justice for everyone.

Jews believe that if everyone were to take notice of the advice in the Torah to "love your neighbor as you love yourself" (Leviticus 19:18) then everything would be well in the world. People, however, have been given free will by God, and many choose not to obey God's laws. The Torah says that those who break these laws must be held responsible for their actions. When they are punished, Jews believe that people are not only paying for their crimes but also acting as deterrents to other possible criminals.

The Death Penalty

The ultimate punishment for the most serious crimes is death, and the Torah lists those crimes for which the punishment should be death by hanging or stoning. As the Torah says: "The principle is a life for a life" (Leviticus 24:17-18). This statement means that if someone takes the life of another he

should surrender his own. In fact, although this was laid down in the Torah, people were rarely put to death in ancient Israel. A murderer could only be executed if there were two independent witnesses to the crime that he or she had committed—and only if the murderer fully understood the consequences of his or her actions. These conditions were usually difficult, and often impossible, to meet.

Modern Israel abolished the death penalty for almost all crimes in the 1950s. Only one person has been executed since 1948, when

Choosing Judges

These standards are set down for judges in the Torah:
"Appoint judges and officials for each of your tribes in every town the Lord your God is giving you, and they shall judge the people fairly. Do not pervert justice or show partiality. Do not accept a bribe, for a bribe blinds the eyes of the wise and twists the words of the righteous. Follow justice and justice alone, so that you may live and possess the land the Lord your God is giving you."

(Deuteronomy 16:18-20)

the modern State of Israel was set up. This happened in 1963, when Adolf Eichmann, a leading Nazi, was publically tried in Jerusalem and found guilty of murdering thousands of Jews during the Holocaust in World War II (*see page 16*). He was executed because his crime was considered so horrific that only the death sentence was suitable.

Remembering the Holocaust

When World War II ended in 1945, and the Allied soldiers liberated the survivors of the Nazi death camps (see page 42), the horror of the Holocaust was revealed to the world. People were deeply shocked. As the truth of the mass murders was gradually pieced together, both Jews and non-Jews became extremely concerned that these events should never be forgotten. In this way it was hoped that the Holocaust could never happen to anyone again.

▼ *The Jewish Museum in Berlin was designed by architect Daniel Libeskind, a Polish Jew, and opened in 2001. The building is in the shape of a long zig-zag, partly based on the idea of an opened Star of David. It celebrates the achievements of German Jews and also commemorates the Holocaust and the millions who died under Nazi rule.*

Anti-Semitism and Racism

For centuries, Jews have found themselves to be the victims of prejudice (*see page 15*). In the case of Jews this prejudice is called anti-Semitism—hatred directed against Jews simply because they are Jews. Jews have often found themselves to be the focus of jokes about their religious traditions, beliefs, ways of worshiping, and clothing. In more extreme cases, Jewish graves, shops, and synagogues have been defaced, vandalized, and attacked. In recent years, anti-Semitism has increased noticeably in Europe.

Racism

Prejudice is not something that happens only to Jews. Many groups of people suffer from prejudice—the disabled, the old, homosexuals, and black people among them. They are often picked on because they are in some way "different" and stand out from other people. At its worst, prejudice can grow into hatred, harassment, and violence. When it involves hatred of a whole race it is called "racism."

Foreigners

This advice comes from the Torah: "When an alien [foreigner] lives with you in your land, do not ill-treat him. The alien living with you must be treated as one of your native-born. Love him as yourself, for you were aliens in Egypt. I am the Lord your God."
(Leviticus 19:33-34)

Jews believe that racism is wrong because all people were created and so are valued by God. They believe that to discriminate against a person is to deny that the person is part of God's good creation. As the Torah says: "God created human beings, making them to be like himself" (Genesis 1:27).

Jews believe that if people are made by God, and are like God, it is wrong to hate them. If all people have been created to serve God in their own different ways then all religions, and people, must be accepted for what they are. The teachings of the Torah explained this long ago and, having often been the victims of persecution themselves, Jews strongly believe that it is wrong to mistreat anyone just because he or she is different.

◄ *Young Jewish prisoners in Dachau concentration camp in Germany cheer their U.S. liberators at the end of World War II, in May 1945.*

In Our Own Words

"I am a Jew. Other people know that I am a Jew and they accept me for what I am. That goes for all my friends. I have not suffered from anti-Semitism, but I do know people who have. I have also read in the newspapers of anti-Semitic acts that have been carried out in many other countries. This worries me a lot. I do not understand why people can't leave us alone. Why do many people hate the Jews so much? Our being different from other people should not be that hard for them to accept."

▼ A woman looks at desecrated Jewish graves at a cemetery in St. Petersburg, Russia, in February 2004. In this attack, the grave stones were daubed with the swastika symbol used by the Nazis. Anti-Semitism has been on the rise in many European countries in recent years.

Wealth and Poverty

The simple fact that some people are very rich while others have barely enough to survive has always upset people. The Torah, though, is quite realistic about this (*see box*). Jews believe that it is God who decides who will be rich and who will be poor. They believe that there will always be rich and poor people in the world.

The Rich and the Poor

In the Jewish Scriptures, it is acceptable for some people to be rich, but it is not acceptable for them to dedicate themselves simply to making more and more money. Judaism teaches that everyone has a duty to help the poor, since no one chooses to be poor. As the Talmud teaches: "Poverty is worse than fifty plagues." At festival times, money should be given so that the poor can join in with the celebrations as well. The Scriptures also give practical advice as to how the poor could be helped and slaves freed in ancient times. They say that at harvest time farmers should leave corn growing at the edges of their fields for the poor to collect. Fruits and olives that were missed at the first picking, should be left. Every seventh year, when a field is left fallow, poor people and wildlife can take what grows. Any slaves must be given their freedom after they have served their masters for six years.

The Poor in Jewish Scriptures

"There will always be poor people in the land. Therefore I command you to be open-handed toward your brothers and toward the poor and needy in your land." (Deuteronomy 15:11)

"When God gives any man wealth and possessions and enables him to enjoy them, to accept his lot and be happy in his work—this is a gift of God." (Ecclesiastes 5:19)

"Naked a man comes from his mother's womb, and as he comes, so he departs. He takes nothing from his labor that he can carry in his hand." (Ecclesiastes 5:15)

▼ The money collected in Jewish charity boxes used to be saved to buy land in Israel but now is mostly used to provide clean drinking water and other services for that country.

Tzedaka

The teaching of the Jewish Scriptures is that everyone should give 10 percent of one's income (a tithe) to the poor. Even someone who has received charity because he or she is poor is expected to give part of it away to other poor people. The word *tzedaka* literally means "justice," and giving a tithe is a fair and right thing to do. No one likes receiving charity in person, so Jews usually give their tzedaka to an organized charity. Then poor people person can receive their rightful share of God's goodness without knowing who gave them the money. It is very important in the Jewish community that the poor should retain their self-respect at all times.

Operation Solomon

For centuries, a community of up to 500,000 Jews lived in the northern province of Gondar in Ethiopia, isolated from the rest of the Jewish world. This community called itself Beta Israel—*the "house of Israel." In the seventeenth century, Beta Israel fought for its independence from Christian Ethiopians, but without success. Only in the nineteenth century did Beta Israel start to make links with the worldwide community of Jews. In the 1970s, anti-Semitism became an increasing problem in Gondar, and many Jews wanted to leave for Israel but were prevented by the Ethiopian government. Terrible famines in Ethiopia in the 1980s led Israel to mount several "rescue" operations for Ethiopian Jews, who are called Falashas. In 1984 and 1985, almost 8,000 Jews were rescued and brought to Israel. In the following five years, more Jews were brought from Ethiopia, but nearly all of those left behind were elderly, women, and children. Then, in 1991, as rebel forces threatened the Ethiopian capital Addis Ababa, a secret Israeli airlift rescued over 14,000 Jews from Ethiopia. This was known as Operation Solomon. There are now 36,000 Ethiopian Jews living in Israel.*

➤ *An Israeli leads a group of Ethiopian Jews to a waiting plane at Addis Ababa airport on May 25 ,1991, during Operation Solomon. The Israeli government authorized a special permit for the Israeli airline, El Al, in order for the airlift to take place on the Jewish Sabbath.*

Glossary

Abraham the patriarch who was the first to believe in one God instead of many gods or idols. He was given the promise by God that his descendants would inherit the land of Israel.

anti-Semitism hatred and prejudice directed toward people because they are Jews

Ark the cabinet in a synagogue in which the Torah is kept

bar mitzvah ("son of the commandment") the ceremony in the synagogue to mark the time when a Jewish boy becomes an adult—after his thirteenth birthday. The boy reads from the Torah in Hebrew and starts to wear his tefillin for daily prayer.

bat mitzvah ("daughter of the commandment") the ceremony in the synagogue to mark a girl's entry into adulthood

bimah the reading-desk in a synagogue from which the Torah is read and the sermon delivered on the Sabbath day

chuppah a canopy under which a wedding service takes place, symbolizing the home that the couple are setting up together

covenant the agreement made between God and Abraham upon which Judaism is based

Diaspora communities of Jews who scattered after the Babylonian exile and settled in many lands outside Palestine

Exodus the journey of the Israelites out of Egyptian slavery toward Canaan, their Promised Land

Halakhah the Jewish legal code that has been drawn up from the Torah

Hanukkah (Festival of Light) a festival that celebrates the victory of a Jewish family called the Maccabees and the miracle of the oil in the Temple

Havdalah the ceremony that marks the end of the Sabbath day

Hebrew the language in which the Jewish Scriptures are written and in which most services in the synagogue are conducted

kaddish a prayer that praises God as the giver of life

ketubah a marriage certificate

kippah a skullcap worn by Orthodox Jewish men

kosher the word applied to the food that Jews are allowed to eat and also to the way in which that food must be prepared

menorah the seven-branched candlestick found in a synagogue

Mesopotamia ("land between two rivers") the ancient region between the Tigris and Euphrates rivers that is today part of modern Iraq

Messiah ("the anointed one") for Jews, a great leader who will be sent by God to deliver them from their enemies and bring all of the world to an understanding of God

mezuzah a casing that holds a tiny scroll on which is written the first two paragraphs of the Shema. A mezuzah is attached to the right-hand door post of most rooms in a Jewish house

mohel the Jewish professional employed to circumcise Jewish boys on the eighth day after birth

Moses the man who led the Israelites out of slavery and received the Torah from God on Mount Sinai

Passover (Pesach) a festival that commemorates the delivery of the Israelites out of Egypt

patriarch one of three founding fathers of the Jewish people: Abraham, Isaac, and Jacob

prophet someone who is believed to have received messages from God

Purim a festival that celebrates the story of Esther, who foiled a plot to destroy the Jewish people about 2,500 years ago

Rabbi the title given to an authorized teacher in Judaism

Rosh Hashanah the Jewish New Year and the start of the Ten Days of Penitence

Sabbath day (Shabbat) the seventh day of the week, the day rest. In the Jewish Bible, it is the day on which God rested from creating the world and a weekly reminder of God's rescuing the Israelites from Egyptian slavery.

seder the special meal that forms the main part of Passover

Shavuot a festival that celebrates the giving of the Torah by God to Moses

Shekhina God's presence or closeness.

Shema ("hear") The Hebrew name for the words of Deuteronomy 6:4.; recited twice each day by Jews as a statement of their faith in God

shofar a ram's horn trumpet

Sukkot a festival that commemorates the time that the Jews spent traveling through the wilderness to their "Promised Land" of Canaan

synagogue the Jewish house of worship; the Jewish meeting place for prayer, study, and instruction in the Scriptures

tallith a prayer shawl

tefillin small boxes containing biblical texts which are bound to the foreheads and left arms of Jewish men (and, in some congregations, women) during prayer

Temple the Jewish Temple in Jerusalem that was first built by Solomon around 950 B.C.E. and destroyed by the Babylonians in 586 B.C.E.

Ten Commandments the law code delivered, according to Jewish belief, by God to Moses on Mount Sinai; the first four commandments are religious laws, and the other six are social

Tenakh the name given to the Jewish Scriptures made up of the Torah, the Prophets, and the Writings

Torah a term Jews use to mean two different things: It can be translated as "law" when it applies particularly to the "law of Moses"—the first five books of the Jewish Scriptures; it can also be used to mean "teaching."

tzedaka ("justice") the act of giving money to those less fortunate in the form of anonymous charity

Yom Kippur the Day of Atonement that brings Rosh Hashanah to a close

Zionist the movement in the nineteenth and twentieth centuries that strived to found a Jewish state in Palestine

Time Line

B.C.E.	
2000-1900	Time of the Biblical patriarchs—Abraham, Isaac, and Jacob
1600s	Israelites go into slavery
1200s-1100s	Moses leads the Israelites out of slavery and receives the Torah and the Ten Commandments. The Israelites conquer Canaan
c.1000	King David unites the tribes in Jerusalem
c. 960	Solomon succeeds David and builds the first Temple
c. 920	Solomon dies and his kingdom divides into Israel in the north and Judah in the south
722	Israel conquered by the Assyrians
586	Judah falls to the Babylonians. Temple in Jerusalem destroyed and Jewish population deported
167	Judas Maccabeus leads a revolt against the Greeks
63	Pompey conquers Palestine. Jewish communities spread throughout Roman Empire
40–4	Romans put Herod the Great on the throne of Judea

C.E.	
66–70	Jews revolt against the Romans. Romans destroy the Temple built by Herod the Great in Jerusalem
638	Muslims conquer Jerusalem
1066	Jews settle in England
1290	Jews expelled from England
1306	Jews expelled from parts of France
1348	The Black Death: Jews are blamed and massacred throughout Europe
1492	Spanish Jews given choice of conversion to Christianity or to leave Spain
1497	Jews expelled from Portugal
1881-2	Jews persecuted in Russia
1917	Balfour Declaration to establish Jewish homeland in Palestine
1939-45	World War II: six million Jews killed in Holocaust
1948	Founding of State of Israel
1967	The "Six-Day War" between Israel and Egypt, Syria, and Jordan
1979	Peace treaty between Israel and Egypt
2005 February	Israeli cabinet approves plan to evacuate groups of Israeli settlers from Palestinian lands, hoping to improve the prospect of peace with Palestinians

Books

Aylett, Liz. *The Jewish Experience*. Hodder and Stoughton, 2000.

Bitton-Jackson, Livia. *I Have Lived a Thousand Years: Growing Up in the Holocaust*. Simon Pulse, Reprint edition, 1999.

Fine, Doreen. *What Do We Know about Judaism?* Hodder Wayland, 1995.

Keene, Michael. *Examining Four Religions*. Harper Collins, 1997.

Matas, Carol. *Daniel's Story*. Scholastic Paperbacks, 1993.

Rush, Barbara, and Cherie Karo Schwartz. *The Kids' Catalogue of Passover*. Jewish Pub. Society of America, 2000.

Web Sites

shamash.org/trb/judaism.html

www.akhlah.com/holidays/hanukkah/hanukkah.php

www.holidays.net/passover/

www.jewfaq.org/alephbet.htm

www.jewishvirtuallibrary.org/jsource/biography/ben_gurion.html

www.jewishvirtuallibrary.org/jsource/Society_&_Culture/kibbutz.html

www.mfa.gov.il/MFA/HomePage

Index